Know your
Dals & Puls

TARLA DALAL
India's # 1 Cookery Author

S&C
SANJAY & CO.
MUMBAI

First Printing : 2008

ISBN : 978-81-89491-75-8

Price: Rs. 89/-

Published & Distributed by : **Sanjay & Company**

353/A-1, Shah & Nahar Industrial Estate, Dhanraj Mill Compound, Lower Parel (W), Mumbai - 400 013. INDIA.

Tel. : (91-22) 2496 8068 • Fax : (91-22) 2496 5876 • E-mail : sanjay@tarladalal.com

Printed by : Minal Sales Agencies, Mumbai

Recipe Research & Production Design
Arati Fedane
Sajani Mathew

Nutritionists
Nisha Katira
Sapna Kamdar

Copy Editor
Janani Gopalakrishnan

Designed by
Satyamangal Rege

Typesetting
Adityas Enterprises

Photography
Nirav Mehta
Jignesh Jhaveri - page 39, 41, 56, 64
Payal Choksi - page 29
Vinay Mahidhar - page 21, 23, 80, 92, 31
Mahesh Hiramath - page 17
Saba Gaziyani - page 13, 95

Dear friends,

Gone are the days when *dals* and pulses were considered a poor man's diet! Today, they have become not just trendy but core to Indian cuisine. Much of the newfound excitement with regard to vegetarian cooking is fuelled by the imaginative use of *dals* and pulses.

The simple, highly-nutritious and comforting *dal-chawal* (lentil-rice) combination is an inseparable part of any traditional, Indian vegetarian meal. The protein-packed super-foods, *dals* and pulses, have been, and continue to be, a part of our culinary tradition across the length and breadth of the country since time immemorial.

But we take these wholesome ingredients so much for granted that very few of us would actually be able to differentiate *toovar dal* from *arhar* and red *chana* from *kala chana*! Well, they are the same, aren't they? We look only at the end-product and think that all dals and pulses look and taste similar; what is there in it! But the surprising fact is that in the raw form *dals* and pulses come in different colours, flavours and with varying degrees of nutrient-content. And it is not at all difficult to understand them; all it takes is a little time and inclination.

Recently, on the 'Ask Tarla' section of our website, I received a query from an 18-year-old who was just foraying into the art of cooking. She wanted to cook *moong dal*, but was faced with three different versions of yellow-coloured dal *toovar*, *chana* and *moong* and she wanted to know which of these was *moong* and how to differentiate it from the other two *dals*. That is when the idea for this book got seeded in my mind.

This book is an effort to introduce you to the world of *dals* and pulses and to demystify the many varieties, so that the next time you go to a shop you can tell the difference between *urad dal* and *moong dal*, and certainly they are two different *dals*! Not to forget the bounty of recipes including *Spicy Urad Dal Puri*, *Masoor Biryani*, *Methi Dal Dhokli* and *Vaal ki Usal*.

Feast healthy!

Regards

Tarla Dalal

AN INTRODUCTION TO THE WORLD OF DALS AND PULSES

An Indian pantry is always stocked with a variety of *dals* and pulses, and rightly so, as it is such an integral part of our cuisine. It is also a power-house of nutrients and when eaten combined with cereals like rice and wheat (as is done traditionally), it is a complete protein supply. Nutritionists say that the amino acids absent in cereals are present in *dals* and pulses; so, when both are combined, they form complete protein. Indeed, our traditional habit is founded on a scientific theory!

Let us explore a little about how *dals* and pulses are stored, washed and sprouted; they are processed; and so on.

PROCESSING OF DALS AND PULSES

FRESH WHOLE BEANS

(Fresh Green *Toovar*, Fresh *Chawli* etc.)

⇩

When the seeds of the beans are dried (Dry *Toovar*, Dry *Chawli*), they are referred to as

PULSES

⇩

When pulses are split, they are referred to as

DALS

Dals with their outer skin *(Chilkewali)*	Dals without their outer skin

Chilkewali dals are nutritionally richer as the skin contains more nutrients as compared to the *dal* without the skin, however both have their own culinary uses.

STORAGE OF DALS AND PULSES

In the days of traditional joint-family, *dals* and pulses were processed or bought in bulk and stored for nearly a year in huge warehouses, store-rooms or containers. Before storing, they were cleaned by removing any stones, dirt and pebbles. After cleaning, they were dried in the sun and oiled or dusted with boric acid to make sure insects and rodents did not infest them. *Dals* and pulses thus home-treated could be preserved yearlong!

But today, due to the emergence of the nuclear family, smaller houses and a fast-paced life, it is not economical or practical to purchase *dals* in bulk and store them year-round. And with groceries being easily available in supermarkets and corner-stores in every locality, people can just buy fresh stock every month! Obviously, life is much easier for us now as *dals* come cleaned and packed. All we need to do is store it in a cool, dry place, in air-tight containers, away from rodents and pests!

PREPARING THE **DALS** AND **PULSES** FOR **COOKING**

Since *dals* and pulses are dried, one needs to follow some simple procedures to prepare them for cooking, the most common steps being washing, soaking and pressure-cooking. Sprouting is another method which not only enhances the taste but also the nutritional content of the pulses. Remember though that *dals* cannot be sprouted, only pulses can.

Picking and washing

Dals and pulses need to be cleaned by placing them in a flat *thali* plate. Small pebbles, shrivelled grains and husk are the commonly-found impurities and they can be removed only by painstakingly picking them out with your fingers. There is absolutely no other way out! After picking, they have to be washed thoroughly in clean water around 2-3 times to remove impurities like dirt, pesticides and preservatives (boric acid).

Soaking

Dals need not be soaked and can be pressure-cooked directly but in order to save on cooking time, 30 minutes of soaking is advised. Remember however that *dals* contain water-soluble vitamins like B-complex which would be lost on soaking, so it is a compromise between speedy cooking or full nutrition it is entirely your call!

Most dried pulses (*chana, vatana, rajma,* etc.) need to be soaked for several hours, sometimes even overnight, to re-hydrate them before cooking because they have a harder outer skin this skin absorbs water over a long time and softens, thus ensuring faster cooking.

Sprouting

Sprouting gives pulses a complete health boost, enhancing their nutrient content and making them easier to digest and absorb. Not just that, the seeds also become crunchier and tastier when sprouted! Remember that almost all pulses can be sprouted but not *dals*. Sprouting time for different pulses is different. To sprout the pulses, spread the soaked pulses on a colander or a sieve and cover with a moist muslin /cotton cloth. Let the seeds sprout over a period of 8 to 16 hours (depending upon the seeds you use). Remember to keep sprinkling water at regular intervals. When your sprouts have grown to the desired length, rinse them again, drain well and then put them in an air-tight container.

URAD

Akha Urad: These are small, oblong, black-skinned beans. When the skin is removed, a creamy white-coloured seed is exposed. It has a strong, musky smell and a rich, heavy taste.

Culinary Uses: This form of *urad* is not used much; nonetheless it does lend itself to some famous recipes such as *dal makhani*. It is especially used in Northern cuisine to make some delicious *dal* where it is known as *"maanh"* and served with oodles of ghee.

Chilkewali Urad Dal:

This is *akha urad* split with the skin on. When they have their outer-skin intact, they are known as *chilkewali urad dal* or skinned split black gram.

Culinary Uses: Again, these are used only in *dals* in northern India. Since *chilkewali dal* is nutritious, one can try using it to make *vadas* and soft *dosas* too!

Urad dal: Also known as white *urad* or split black gram. When they are split, they become creamy-white and smooth. *Urad dal* has a subtle, flour-like smell and a bland taste. It can also be made into flour though it is not very readily available in India.

Culinary Uses: *Urad dal* is used for making the batter for *Dosa, Idlis, Vadas* etc. It is also used for seasoning along with mustard in vegetable dishes like *upma* and a few South Indian curries like *Upkaries, Foogath* etc.

DAL MAKHANI

A rich and luscious variety of dal ideal for a festive meal! One of the most well-known recipes made using whole urad.

Preparation Time: 15 minutes.
Cooking Time: 20 to 25 minutes.
Serves 4.
Soaking Time : Overnight.

¾ cup *akha urad* (whole black gram)
2 tbsp *rajma* (kidney beans)
Salt to taste
3 tbsp butter
1 tsp cumin seeds (*jeera*)
2 green chillies, slit
25 mm. (1") stick cinnamon (*dalchini*)
2 cloves (*laung / lavang*)
3 cardamom (*elaichi*)
½ cup finely chopped onions
½ tsp ginger-garlic (*adrak-lehsun*) paste
1 tsp chilli powder
¼ tsp turmeric powder (*haldi*)

1½ cups blanched and grated tomatoes
¾ cup (150 grams) cream

For the garnish
2 tbsp chopped coriander (*dhania*)
1 tbsp butter

1. Clean, wash and soak the *urad* and *rajma* in enough water overnight.
2. Drain, add salt and 2 cups of water and pressure cook till the *urad* and *rajma* are overcooked.
3. Allow the steam to escape before opening the lid.
4. Whisk well till the *dal* is almost mashed. Keep aside.
5. Heat the butter in a deep pan and add the cumin seeds.
6. When the cumin seeds crackle, add the green chillies, cinnamon, cloves, cardamom, onions and ginger-garlic paste and sauté on a medium flame till the onions turn golden brown in colour.
7. Add the chilli powder, turmeric powder and tomatoes and cook on a medium flame till the oil separates from the gravy.
8. Add the *dal* mixture, ¾ cup of water and salt if required and simmer for 10 to 15 minutes.
9. Add the cream and mix well.

   Serve hot garnished with coriander and butter.

KHATTA URAD DAL

This dal recipe made using chilkewali urad dal is tangy as the name suggests, but the tanginess is mild and only enhances the flavour of this dish.

Preparation Time: 5 minutes.
Cooking Time: 25 minutes.
Serves 4.
Soaking Time : 15 minutes.

Chilkewali Urad Dal

1 cup *chilkewali urad dal* (skinned split black gram)
½ cup sour curds (*khatta dahi*), whisked with 1 cup of water
½ tsp turmeric powder (*haldi*)
1 tsp chilli powder
½ tsp garlic paste
Salt to taste

For the garnish
2 tbsp chopped coriander (*dhania*)

1. Clean, wash and soak the *chilkewali urad dal* in water for about 15 minutes. Drain and keep aside.
2. Drain, add 1½ cups of water and pressure cook for at least 4 whistles.
3. Allow the steam to escape before opening the lid.
4. Add all the remaining ingredients and simmer for 10 minutes.
   Serve hot garnished with coriander.

HANDY TIP

If the curd curdles while boiling, add 1 tsp *besan* (Bengal gram flour) mixed with 2 tbsp of water and mix well. This will help to thicken the *dal*.

SPICY URAD DAL PURIS

Serve these delicious urad dal puris with a sweetish pickle and hot tea on a sunny Sunday morning, to recreate a complete Rajasthani ambience right in your living room!

Preparation Time: 20 minutes.
Cooking Time: 30 minutes
Makes 10 *puris*.
Soaking Time : 4 hours.

For the dough

1½ cups plain flour (*maida*)
½ tsp nigella seeds (*kalonji*)
Salt to taste
2 tbsp hot oil

To be dry roasted and ground into a powder

1 tbsp coriander (*dhania*) seeds
1 tbsp cumin seeds (*jeera*)
1 tsp fennel seeds (*saunf*)
8 black peppercorns
4 whole dry Kashmiri red chillies

For the stuffing

¾ cup *urad dal* (split black gram)
2 tbsp oil
Salt to taste

Other ingredients
Oil or ghee for rolling and deep-frying

For the dough
1. Combine all the ingredients in a bowl and knead into a stiff dough using enough water.
2. Keep aside for 20 minutes.
3. Divide into 10 equal portions. Keep aside.

For the stuffing
1. Clean, wash and soak the *urad dal* in water for 4 hours.
2. Drain and blend in a mixer to a coarse paste using very little water.
3. Heat the oil in a *kadhai*, add the *urad dal* paste and sauté till it turns light golden in colour. Keep aside to cool for 10 minutes.
4. Add the prepared powder and salt and mix well.
5. Divide the stuffing into 10 equal portions and keep aside.

How to proceed
1. Roll out one portion of the dough into a thin round of about 50 mm. (2″) diameter with the help of a little oil.
2. Put one portion of the stuffing in the centre and close the edges to cover the stuffing completely. Roll out again into small *puris* with the help of a little oil.
3. Repeat with the remaining portions and stuffing to make 9 more stuffed *puris*.
4. Heat the oil in a *kadhai* and deep-fry the *puris* a few at a time till they turn golden brown in colour from both sides. Drain on absorbent paper and serve hot.

MOONG

Moong: Also known as whole green gram, these are small green beans that have a musky flavour and a chewy texture.

Culinary Uses: This is an extremely popular sprout and is used in salads and stir-fries. It is also used as a filling in the famous *pani puri*! It also lends itself to making dry subzis. *Khatta Moong* is a famous Gujarati delicacy.

Chilkewali Moong Dal:

Skinned split green gram or *moong dal* with the skin on retains all the B group vitamins during cooking.

Culinary Uses: It is used in a variety of vegetable dishes, and as a stuffing for *parathas*.

Moong dal: The split yellow gram is small and flattish. They are easy to cook and need no soaking. One of the most popular and versatile among the *dals*, it is one of the easiest to cook and digest, and is very popular all over India.

It is also the preferred *dal* when one is experiencing digestion problems as it is easier to digest. In fact, boiled and mashed *moong dal* is recommended for babies as an easily digestible source of protein.

Culinary Uses: Apart from being made into *dal*, the split yellow gram is also used to make *Khichdi, Dal, Barfi, Payasam* and other sweets.

MOONG SPROUTS PAV BHAJI

I am sure this new version of pav bhaji using moong sprouts is sure to win a good share of fans just like the original! Relish the bhaji with chapati to morph a regular meal into a healthy fare.

Preparation Time: 10 minutes.
Cooking Time: 20 minutes.
Serves 4.

3 tbsp butter
½ cup boiled onion paste, refer handy tip
2 cups tomato purée
2 tsp chilli powder
1 tbsp *pav bhaji masala*
Salt to taste
1 cup boiled, peeled and mashed potatoes
½ cup chopped and boiled mixed vegetables (carrots, cauliflower, green peas), mashed
1½ cups *moong* (whole green gram) sprouts
2 tbsp chopped coriander (*dhania*)

For the garnish
2 tbsp chopped coriander (*dhania*)
2 tbsp chopped onions
1 tbsp butter

For serving
8 *laddi pav*

1. Heat the butter in a *kadhai*, add the onion paste and sauté till it turns light brown in colour.
2. Add the tomatoes, chilli powder, *pav bhaji masala* and salt and simmer for 5 to 7 minutes, stirring once in between.
3. Add the potatoes, mixed vegetables, *moong* sprouts and 1 cup water and simmer for another 8 to 10 minutes, while stirring continuously.
4. Garnish with coriander, onions and butter and serve with *laddi pav*.

HANDY TIP

To get ½ cup of boiled onion paste, combine 2 cups of chopped onions with ¾ cup of water and boil till the onions turn translucent. Cool and blend in a mixer to a fine paste.

STUFFED MOONG DAL CHILAS

Set your imagination free and experiment with these interesting chilkewali moong dal chilas. You can change the stuffing to suit your taste, perhaps you'll fall in love with a filling of stir-fried vegetables with soya sauce!

For the *chila* batter

2 cups *chilkewali moong dal* (skinned split green gram)
2 tsp finely chopped green chillies
A pinch asafoetida (*hing*)
Salt to taste

For the stuffing

1 tbsp oil
1 tsp cumin seeds (*jeera*)
2 tsp finely chopped green chillies
1 cup boiled potato cubes
2 cups boiled green peas
1 tbsp dried mango powder (*amchur*)
Salt to taste

Preparation Time: 15 minutes.
Cooking Time: 40 minutes.
Makes 15 *chilas*.
Soaking Time: 3 hours.

Other ingredients

Oil for greasing and cooking

For the *chila* batter

1. Clean, wash and soak the *chilkewali moong dal* in water for at least 3 hours.
2. Drain, add the green chillies, asafoetida, salt and enough water and blend in a mixer to a coarse paste and keep aside.

For the stuffing

1. Heat the oil in a *kadhai* and add the cumin seeds.
2. When the seeds crackle, add all the remaining ingredients and cook for a few minutes.
3. Mash lightly, divide the stuffing into 15 equal portions and keep aside.

How to proceed

1. Heat a non-stick pan and grease it with oil.
2. Pour a ladleful of the *chila* batter on the pan and spread it evenly to make a thin of 25 mm (5″) diameter circle.
3. Cook the *chila* using a little oil till brown spots appear on both sides.
4. Place one portion of the stuffing on one half of the *chila* and fold to make a semi-circle.
5. Repeat with the remaining batter and stuffing to make 14 more stuffed *chilas*.
   Serve hot.

MOONG DAL SHEERA

Inseparable from Gujarati and Rajasthani cuisine, this moong dal dish is a great value-add for any festive fare! Remember to cook the dal for a long time on a low flame.

Preparation Time : 10 minutes.
Cooking Time : 40 minutes.
Serves 4.
Soaking Time : 3 to 4 hours.

Yellow Moong Dal

1 cup yellow *moong dal* (split yellow gram)
A few strands of saffron (*kesar*)
1 cup milk, warmed
6 tbsp ghee
1¼ cups sugar
½ tsp cardamom (*elaichi*) powder

For the garnish
Almond (*badam*) and pistachio slivers
A few strands of saffron (*kesar*)

1. Clean, wash and soak the *moong dal* in water for 3 to 4 hours.
2. Drain and blend in a mixer to a coarse paste using very little water. Keep aside.
3. Dissolve the saffron in 1 tbsp of warm milk and keep aside.
4. Heat the ghee in a broad non-stick pan, add the *moong dal* paste and cook on a medium flame till it becomes golden brown in colour, while stirring continuously.
5. Add the remaining warm milk and 1 cup of warm water and cook on a medium flame, while stirring continuously, till all the liquid is absorbed.
6. Add the sugar and cook on a slow flame till the ghee separates, while stirring continuously.
7. Add the saffron and cardamom powder and mix well.

   Serve hot garnished with almond and pistachio slivers and saffron strands.

CHANA

Chana or chick peas comes in many varieties, each looking and tasting different, and lending themselves to a wide range of dishes. Let us take a detailed look at these many types of *chana*.

Types of chana:

Kabuli chana: Also known as white chick peas, *kabuli chana* is extremely popular all over India, and even in Pakistan and Bangladesh. It belongs to the pea family, and is hard and creamy-white, with a thick skin that often comes away while soaking and cooking. It has a nutty and bland taste.

Culinary uses: Cooked *kabuli chana* lends itself to a wide range of *pulaos* and *subzis*. The popular Punjabi dish *Chole* needs no introduction it is made with white chick peas in a gravy blended with an array of spices. Lebanese cuisine too is incomplete without these chick peas; the famous Hummus is an example of a dish made with white chick peas. *Kabuli chana* is also used to prepare Potato and *Chana* Salad, Three-bean Salad etc.

Hara chana:

They are also known as green chick peas. As the name suggests, they are dark green in colour and small as compared to *kabuli chana*. The tender *chana* can be eaten raw as is, or roasted a lovely pastime for a rainy day!

Culinary uses: Green *chana* is used to make the ever-popular street food *hare chane ka chaat*. It is also used to make spicy curries like *masala chana*. Can also be boiled and used in salads.

Kala chana:

Also known as brown chick peas, these are small, hard and dark in colour, with a thick skin. When raw, *kala chana* has a strong, earthy aroma, and once cooked it acquires a nutty flavour. Black chick peas can also be sprouted.

Culinary uses: These beans retain their shape and are therefore a good addition to salads. They can be sautéed slightly and mixed with freshly chopped onions and lime juice, to make a delicious, simple side-dish. They can also be cooked with or without salt, sautéed in garlic butter or mayonnaise and mixed with lightly-cooked vegetables to make a scrumptious salad. If you like them spicier, no problem, they also taste excellent when made into a hot, spicy curry garnished with grated coconut. Not to forget the popular Maharashtrian dish, *Amti*, made with *kala chana*. Black chick pea sprouts can be used to make *pulao*. In all, a versatile ingredient!

Chana dal:

The split and de-husked relative of chick peas, *chana dal* (split Bengal gram) is, arguably, the most popular legume in India. Made by splitting *kala chana*. *Chana dal* is slightly bigger and coarser than *toovar dal;* it is also stronger in taste than most *dals* with a nutty-sweet aroma and flavour.

Culinary uses: The delicious, nutritious and easily-digestible *chana dal* can be cooked in various ways: in dal dishes and savouries, as well as in sweets. It is often stewed with vegetables, especially bitter gourd. They can also be combined with tomatoes, garlic and onions to make curries, or mixed with vegetables to make *koftas* and *kebabs*. The *dals* are also roasted and powdered into *besan* (Bengal gram flour). They lend themselves to sweets like *besan ladoo* and *puran poli*. In fact, Bengal gram is associated with festivals. One of the highlights of the Onam festival of Kerala is the *Chana Dal Payasam*, a traditional kheer made with *chana dal*, jaggery, coconut, cardamom, cashewnuts and raisins.

PESHAWARI CHOLE

One of Peshawar's cultural contributions to this world is its luscious cuisine. Peshawari Chole is a characteristic dish, very popular in Punjab. Spicy and 'chatpata', this dish needs some prior planning as the chick peas require soaking for at least 6 hours.

Preparation Time: 15 minutes.
Cooking Time: 1 hour. Serves 4.
Soaking Time : Overnight.

1 cup *kabuli chana* (white chick peas)
1 tbsp *chana dal* (split Bengal gram)
2 big cardamom (*moti elaichi*)
25 mm. (1") stick cinnamon (*dalchini*)
1 teabag
4 tbsp oil
1 cup chopped onions
1½ tsp pomegranate (*anardana*) seeds roasted and powdered
1 cup chopped tomatoes
1 tbsp finely chopped ginger (*adrak*)
2 tsp finely chopped green chillies
1 tsp coriander (*dhania*) powder
½ tsp chilli powder
½ tsp *garam masala*
1 tsp *chole masala*
Salt to taste

1. Clean, wash and soak the *kabuli chana* and *chana dal* in enough water overnight or for 6-8 hours.
2. Drain, wash again, add 2 cups of water, big cardamom, cinnamon and teabags and pressure cook for 1 whistle.
3. Reduce the flame and cook for 20 minutes.
4. Allow the steam to escape before opening the lid.
5. Strain and reserve the liquid but discard the tea bag. Keep the *kabuli chana* liquid aside separately.
6. Heat the oil in a *kadhai,* add the onions and sauté till they turn translucent, while stirring continuously.
7. Add the pomegranate seed powder and cook, till the onions turn dark brown while stirring continuously.
8. Add the tomatoes, ginger and green chillies and cook on a medium flame for 3-4 minutes.
9. Add the coriander powder, chilli powder and *garam masala* and sauté till the tomatoes are cooked and the mixture leaves oil.
10. Add the cooked *kabuli chana, chole masala,* the reserved liquid and a little salt if required and mix gently.
11. Cook for 15-20 minutes on a slow flame till some of the liquid dries up.
    Serve hot with *puris.*

HARA CHANA CURRY WITH METHI MUTHIA

All time favourite methi muthias innovatively cooked using hara chana and a coconut gravy.

Preparation Time: 15 minutes.
Cooking Time: 15 minutes.
Serves 4.

To be ground into a smooth paste

½ cup chopped coriander (*dhania*)
3 to 4 green chillies
12 mm. (½") piece ginger (*adrak*)
3 cloves garlic (*lehsun*)
1 tsp lemon juice
3 to 4 spinach (*palak*) leaves
1 tbsp of water

For the *hara chana* curry

1 tbsp oil
¼ cup chopped onions
½ cup *hara chana*, soaked overnight and boiled
½ tsp cornflour dissolved in 2 cups coconut milk
Salt to taste
2 tbsp chopped coriander (*dhania*) for the garnish

For the *methi muthias*

1 cup chopped *methi* (fenugreek) leaves
$^1/_3$ cup whole wheat flour (*gehun ka atta*)
2 tbsp *besan* (Bengal gram flour)
A pinch asafoetida
1 tsp sugar
1 tsp green chilli-ginger paste
1 tbsp hot oil
Oil for deep frying

For the *methi muthias*

1. Combine all the ingredients together in a bowl and mix well. Divide it into 15 to 20 equal portions and shape each into round balls.
2. Deep the balls in hot oil in the batches of 10 to 12 on a slow flame till they turn golden brown in colour.
3. Drain on an absorbent paper and keep aside.

For the *hara chana* curry

1. Heat the oil in a *kadhai*, add the onions and sauté on a medium flame till they turn translucent.
2. Add the prepared paste, mix well and sauté on a medium flame for 2 to3 minutes, while stirring continuously.
3. Add the boiled *chana* and cornflour and coconut mixture, mix well and simmer for another 5 minutes or till the curry thickens, stirring once in between. Keep aside.

How to proceed

Just before serving, add the prepared *methi muthias* to the *hara chana* curry and simmer for 2 to 3 minutes.
Serve immediately garnished with coriander.

SUNDAL

Sundal is a simple, tasty and extremely popular South Indian snack. Extremely healthy, this is an indispensable part of the Navratri (Dusshera) celebrations in Tamilnadu. As a contemporary variation, you can stir-fry it with rice, to make a main course meal of it!

Preparation Time: 10 minutes.
Cooking Time: 25 minutes.
Serves 4.
Soaking Time: Overnight.

Kala Chana

1 cup *kala chana* (brown chick peas)
1 tbsp coconut oil/ any other refined oil
1 tsp mustard seeds (*rai / sarson*)
1 tsp *urad dal* (split black gram)
1 whole dry Kashmiri red chilli, broken into pieces
½ tsp asafoetida (*hing*)
½ cup finely chopped raw mangoes (optional)
2 tbsp freshly grated coconut
Salt to taste

1. Clean, wash and soak the *kala chana* in enough water overnight. Next morning, drain and keep aside.
2. Combine the *kala chana* with 2 cups of water and pressure cook for 4 to 5 whistles.
3. Allow the steam to escape before opening the lid. Keep aside.
4. Heat the oil in a *kadhai* and add the mustard seeds.
5. When the seeds crackle, add the *urad dal*, red chillies and asafoetida and sauté on a medium flame till the *dal* turns light brown in colour.
6. Add the *kala chana*, mangoes, coconut and salt, mix well and cook on a medium flame for another 4 to 5 minutes, while stirring continuously.
7. Remove from the flame and serve hot.

DAL PAKWAN

A soothing dal made with chana dal accompanied by pakwans, is a traditional favourite with Sindhis. It makes for a wholesome breakfast!

Preparation Time : 20 minutes.
Cooking Tme : 40 minutes.
Serves 6.
Soaking Time : 3 to 4 hours.

For the *dal*

1¼ cups *chana dal* (split Bengal gram)
2 tbsp ghee or oil
1 tsp cumin seeds (*jeera*)
½ cup finely chopped onions
2 green chillies, slit
½ tsp turmeric powder (*haldi*)
Salt to taste
1 large tomato, finely chopped
1 tsp coriander-cumin seed (*dhania-jeera*) powder
½ tsp chilli powder
2 tbsp chopped coriander (*dhania*)
¼ tsp *garam masala*

For the *pakwans*

2 cups plain flour (*maida*)
1 cup whole wheat flour (*gehun ka atta*)
1 tsp cumin seeds (*jeera*)

Salt to taste
Oil for deep-frying

For serving
6 tbsp chopped onions
6 tbsp green *chutney*

For the *dal*

1. Clean, wash and soak the *chana dal* in enough water for 3 to 4 hours. Drain and keep aside.
2. Heat the ghee in a deep pan and add the cumin seeds.
3. When the seeds crackle, add the onions and chillies and sauté till the onions turn light brown in colour.
4. Add the *chana dal*, turmeric powder, salt and ½ cup of water and cover and cook on a slow flame for 15 to 20 minutes or till the *dal* is soft.
5. Add the tomatoes, coriander-cumin seed powder, chilli powder and coriander and cook for 1 minute. Sprinkle the *garam masala* on top and keep aside.

For the *pakwans*

1. Combine the plain flour, wheat flour, cumin seeds and salt and knead into a stiff dough using enough water.
2. Divide the dough into 18 equal portions and roll each portion into 125 mm. (5") diameter circle.
3. Prick each circle with a fork.
4. Heat the oil in a *kadhai* and deep-fry the pakwans, one at a time, till they are golden brown in colour. Drain on absorbent paper and keep aside.

How to proceed

Serve the hot *dal* with the *pakwans*, onions and *chutney*.

MASOOR

Masoor : Also called whole red lentil, these are dark brown or greenish-brown in colour, with a pinkish-orange centre. They are musky, coarse and chewy.

Culinary uses: They can be used to make delicious *biryani* and are also used in vegetable preparations. While a South Indian will flavour it with tamarind and curry leaves, a North Indian is likely to blend it with *garam masala* and tomatoes, but there is no denying *masoor* its rightful presence in almost every Indian kitchen. You can replace plain *masoor* with sprouted *masoor* in *pulaos, biryanis,* dry and gravy-based *subzis* and any such recipe that calls for *masoor*. The taste will not be affected or altered but the nutrient content will be enhanced considerably.

Masoor dal : De-husked split red lentils are orange in colour and have a distinctive earthy and nutty flavour and creamy texture. These seeds have a short cooking time and so they need not be soaked. They are also easy to digest.

Culinary uses: These lentils combine well with tomatoes and may be served on their own as a side dish, or incorporated into soups, salads, and *dals*. A variety of *dals* can be prepared using *masoor dal*, such as *Hariyali Dal, Dal Pinni, Masala Masoor dal* etc.

MASOOR BIRYANI

Masoor spells iron shakthi, which is very important for building haemoglobin levels and to ward off fatigue and tiredness. Here is an interesting biryani made using this nutritious ingredient. Make the rice in advance to save time and effort. I have added apricots and raisins to the masoor masala to make it more interesting.

Preparation Time: 15 minutes.
Cooking Time: 10 minutes.
Serves 4.
Soaking Time: 1-2 hours.
Baking Temperature: 200°C (400°C).
Baking Time: 15 minutes.

For the *masala masoor*

1 tbsp oil
½ cup *masoor* (whole red lentils), soaked for 1-2 hours
½ cup chopped onions
3 tbsp red chilli-garlic paste
½ cup potato cubes
¾ cup chopped tomatoes
2 apricots (*jardalu / kummani*), soaked and finely chopped
1 tbsp chopped raisins (*kismis*)
Salt to taste

Other ingredients

2½ cups cooked rice (*chawal*)
Oil for greasing

For the garnish

2 tbsp chopped coriander (*dhania*)

For the *masala masoor*

1. Clean, wash and soak the *masoor* in enough water atleast 1 to 2 hours. Drain the *masoor*. Keep aside.
2. Heat the oil in a pressure cooker add the onions and sauté till they turn brown in colour, while stirring continuously.
3. Add the red chilli-garlic paste and sauté for a few more seconds, while stirring continuously.
4. Add the potatoes, tomatoes, apricots, raisins, *masoor*, salt and 1¼ cups of water and pressure cook for 1 whistle.
5. Allow the steam to escape before opening the lid.
6. If it is watery, simmer till little moisture evaporates and the mixture becomes semi-dry. Keep aside.

How to proceed

1. Divide the rice into 3 equal portions and the *masala masoor* into 2 equal portions keep aside.
2. Spread one portion of the rice in an even layer in a greased glass baking dish.
3. Spread one portion of the *masala masoor* over it.
4. Spread the remaining rice over the *masala masoor* in an even layer. Repeat the steps 2 and 3 to make one more layer.
5. Cover with an aluminium foil and bake in a pre-heated oven at 200°C (400°F) for 10 minutes or microwave for 2 minutes. Ensure you do not use aluminium foil while microwaving, as it may cause a spark. Use a microwave-safe lid instead.
6. Turn upside down on a large serving plate, just before serving. Serve hot garnished with coriander.

HEARTY RED LENTIL SOUP

There is an unmistakable Turkish influence in this soup. Made with the humble red lentil, this soup is more than a soup! It can even serve as a main dish. Rice gives body to the soup and milk tones down the strong flavour of lentils even while making the soup richer and creamier.

Preparation Time: 5 minutes.
Cooking Time: 20 minutes.
Serves 4.

¼ cup mint leaves (*phudina*)
½ cup *masoor dal* (split red lentils)
½ cup rice (*chawal*)
¾ cup roughly chopped onions
¾ cup roughly chopped carrots
1 tomato, roughly chopped
¼ cup milk
¼ tsp dry red chilli flakes (paprika)
Salt to taste
A few mint leaves (*phudina*) for the garnish

1. Heat a small non-stick pan and when hot, add the mint leaves and dry roast till they are crisp. Crush them slightly and keep aside.
2. Clean, wash and drain the *masoor dal* and rice.
3. Add the onions, carrots, tomatoes and 2 cups of water and pressure cook for 2 whistles.
4. Allow the steam to escape before opening the lid.
5. Blend in a mixer till smooth.
6. Transfer to a pan, add ½ cup of water, milk, chilli flakes, roasted mint leaves and salt and simmer for a few minutes.

   Serve hot garnished with mint leaves.

TOOVAR

Toovar:

Also called "whole arhar", these lentils are black when whole, and have a distinct flavour. They are, unfortunately, not very well-known. They need to be soaked overnight.

Culinary uses: Maharashtrians make *Usal* and *Amti* using whole *toovar*. Gujaratis also use it in their cooking, and Mangaloreans make *Ghassi* with it.

Toovar dal: Every Indian eats *dal* otherwise called "*arhar dal*" daily and the Hindi term *dal-roti* has become a clichéd phrase meaning everyday food. *Dals* are literally prepared in thousands of ways all over India. The *toovar dal* is perhaps one of the most versatile of these; it can be made into innumerable dishes ground into paste, crushed into sweets, and added whole to vegetables for flavour and texture. *Toovar dal* has a mild, nutty flavour, and is easy to cook.

Culinary uses: *Toovar dal* is used to make spicy dishes and combines well with spices and vegetables. They can be transformed into a number of dishes roasted, ground or added whole to vegetables. *Toovar dal* is very popular in Southern and Western India. The famous Gujarati dish *Methi Dal Dhokli* is made using *toovar dal*. *Toovar dal* cooked the Maharashtrian way acquires a sweet and sour taste and is popularly known as *Amti*. The South Indian sambar, made using *toovar dal*, of course, needs no introduction. Mudda pappu or pressure cooked *toovar dal*, mashed and salted, is served as the first course in a traditional Andhra meal. It is eaten mixed with hot steamed white rice and a dollop of *ghee*.

MASALA TOOVAR

A tasty, slightly-spicy side-dish made with whole toovar. This goes well with any type of roti or paratha.

Preparation Time : 10 minutes.
Cooking Time : 35 minutes.
Serves 6.
Soaking Time : Overnight.

To be ground into a paste
8 cloves garlic (*lehsun*)
8 whole dry red chillies
2 tsp coriander (*dhania*) seeds
1 tsp cumin seeds (*jeera*)
35 mm. (1½") piece ginger (*adrak*)

Other ingredients
1 cup *toovar* (whole red gram/*arhar*), soaked overnight
7 to 8 small whole onions
4 tbsp ghee
1 cup sliced onions
Salt to taste
¾ cup chopped tomatoes

For the garnish
2 tbsp chopped coriander (*dhania*)

1. Clean, wash and soak the *toovar* in enough water overnight, add 2½ cups of water and the whole onions and pressure cook for 2 to 3 whistles or till the *toovar* is cooked.
2. Allow the steam to escape before opening the lid. Keep aside.
3. Heat the ghee in a *kadhai*, add the sliced onions and sauté for 2 to 3 minutes, while stirring continuously.
4. Add the ground paste and sauté for another 3 to 4 minutes, while stirring continuously.
5. Add the cooked *toovar*, 1 cup of water and salt, mix well and simmer for 5 minutes, stirring once in between.
6. Add the tomatoes and simmer for another 10 minutes.
   Serve hot garnished with coriander.

METHI DAL DHOKLI

Dhoklis, simmered in toovar dal need no introduction to those familiar with Gujarati cuisine. This is a slightly modified variant of dhokli, to which I have added methi.

Preparation Time: 20 minutes.
Cooking Time: 45 minutes.
Serves 4.
Soaking Time : 2 to 3 hours.

For the *dal*

½ cup *toovar dal* (split red gram / *arhar dal*)
1 tsp oil
1 tsp ghee
¼ tsp mustard seeds (*rai* / *sarson*)
¼ tsp cumin seeds (*jeera*)
¼ tsp fenugreek (*methi*) seeds
10 curry leaves (*kadipatta*)
2 cloves (*laung* / *lavang*)
2 sticks cinnamon (*dalchini*)
1 bayleaf (*tejpatta*)
2 small round red chillies (*boriya mirchi*)
¼ tsp asafoetida (*hing*)
4 to 5 *kokum*, soaked in ¼ cup water
1 tbsp peanuts
¼ cup chopped tomatoes
½ tsp turmeric powder (*haldi*)
Juice of ½ lemon
4 green chillies, slit
½ tsp chilli powder
1 tsp grated ginger (*adrak*)
2 tbsp grated jaggery (*gur*)
Salt to taste

For the *dhoklis*

1 cup whole wheat flour (*gehun ka atta*)
¾ cup chopped fenugreek (*methi*) leaves
½ tsp turmeric powder (*haldi*)
½ tsp chilli powder
¼ tsp asafoetida (*hing*)
1 tsp oil
¼ tsp carom seeds (*ajwain*)
Salt to taste

For the garnish

¼ cup chopped coriander (*dhania*)

For the *dal*

1. Wash and soak the *dal* in enough water for a 2 to 3 hours. Add 4 cups of water and pressure cook till the *dal* is cooked. Keep aside.
2. When the *dal* is cooked, cool slightly and whisk till it is smooth.
3. Heat the ghee and oil in a deep pan and add the mustard seeds, cumin seeds, fenugreek seeds, curry leaves, cloves, cinnamon, bayleaf, small round chillies and asafoetida and sauté for 30 seconds.
4. Add the cooked *dal*, peanuts, 3 cups of water, *kokum*, tomatoes, turmeric powder, lemon juice, green chillies, chilli powder, ginger and jaggery and simmer for 10 minutes.

For the *dhoklis*

1. Knead all the ingredients together with enough water to make a firm dough.
2. Divide into 6 equal portions and roll out into thin *chapatis*.
3. Heat a non-stick *tava* (griddle) and lightly roast the *chapatis* on both sides. Keep aside.
4. Cut the *chapatis* into diamonds or squares and keep asides.

How to proceed

1. Just before serving, boil the *dal* and slowly add the *dhoklis* and simmer for 15 minutes, while stirring every 2 to 3 minutes.
2. Garnish with the coriander and serve hot.

HANDY TIP

1. Add the *dhoklis* one by one into the *dal* as otherwise they could form one big lump.
2. Add more water if the *dal* thickens while simmering adjust the seasoning too if needed.

VAAL

Vaal (dried): Most commonly known as "field beans" but also sometimes called 'butter beans' because of its starchy and buttery texture. It has a delicate flavour that complements a wide variety of dishes. It is also an excellent source of molybdenum. Dried *vaal* beans are creamy-white to light tan in colour, flat and long. They have a thick white ridge on one side. As *vaal* is quite hard, it is necessary to soak them. Then *vaal* has to be peeled in order to remove the skin and then they are ready to be cooked. It can also be sprouted and used. There are two broad varieties of *vaal: kadva* and *goda*. As the name suggests one is slightly bitter and the other sweetish. One can be interchanged for the other depending on your personal preference.

Culinary uses: *Vaal* tastes very good when blended with coconut, jaggery and ginger. They can also be sprouted and used with vegetables like in the Maharashtrian dish *Vangi Ani Val. Dalimbi* is a very famous traditional Maharashtrian dish.

Vaal Dal: These are split field beans. This cream-coloured, slightly oval shaped *dal* must be soaked before use.

Culinary uses: *Vaal Dal* can be used in *Pulaos, Dals* and vegetable preparations. *Walor Muthia nu Shaak* is a popular Gujarati dish where *val dal* is used along with fenugreek leaves.

Rangoon Vaal or Lilva Beans:

This is a variety of *vaal* which is hard and white in colour. The beans are big and hence also called double beans or broad beans. It must be soaked overnight, and peeled before eating as the skin is very thick.

Culinary uses: Rangoon *vaal* curry made using the typical Punjabi *masala* gives this predominantly Gujarati pulse a radically different hue. *Tittori Dal,* a traditional Parsi *dal* recipe is also made using *Rangoon Vaal.*

VAAL KI USAL

This is a popular, easy-fix Maharashtrian dish. The combination of jaggery and kokum gives a sweet and tangy taste to this usal, which is made using vaal.

Preparation Time : 10 minutes.
Cooking Time : 25 minutes.
Serves 4.
Soaking Time : 15 to 20 minutes.

4 to 5 fresh *kokums*
1 tbsp oil
1 tsp cumin seeds (*jeera*)
½ tsp asafoetida (*hing*)
5 to 6 curry leaves (*kadi patta*)
1 tsp grated ginger (*adrak*)
1 cup finely chopped onions
2 cups soaked *vaal* (field beans)
½ tsp turmeric powder (*haldi*)
3 tsp chopped jaggery (*gur*)
2 tsp chilli powder
4 tbsp chopped coriander (*dhania*)
Salt to taste

1. Soak the *kokum* in ¼ cup of warm water for 15 to 20 minutes.
2. Mash it with your hands and keep aside.
3. Heat the oil in a non-stick *kadhai* and add the cumin seeds.
4. When they crackle, add the asafoetida, curry leaves and ginger and sauté for a few seconds.
5. Add the onions and sauté till they turn translucent, while stirring continuously.
6. Add the *vaal* and 1 cup of water, cover and cook on a medium flame for 15 minutes.
7. Add the turmeric powder, *kokum* mixture, jaggery, chilli powder, coriander and salt and simmer for another 5 minutes, stirring once in between.
   Serve hot.

VAL DAL KHICHDI

One dish meals are quite a rage in this fast-paced world where one has very little time to spend in the kitchen! Here is an easy-to-make and healthy one dish meal using vaal dal.

Preparation Time : 15 minutes.
Cooking Time : 25 minutes.
Serves 4.
Soaking Time : 10 minutes.

Vaal Dal

1 cup *vaal dal* (split field beans)
1 cup rice (*chawal*)
½ cup ghee
½ tsp cumin seeds (*jeera*)
3 to 4 cloves (*laung / lavang*)
2 sticks cinnamon (*dalchini*)
2 bayleaves (*tejpatta*)
1 cup cauliflower florets
¾ cup brinjal (*baingan* / eggplant) cubes
¾ cup potato cubes
¾ cup French beans, cut into 1" pieces
½ cup onion cubes
½ cup green peas
½ tsp turmeric powder (*haldi*)
1 tsp chilli powder
½ tsp *garam masala*
Salt to taste

1. Soak the *vaal dal* and rice in enough water for 10 minutes. Drain and keep aside.
2. Heat the ghee in a pressure cooker and add the cumin seeds, cloves, cinnamon and bayleaves.
3. When the cumin seeds crackle, all the vegetables, turmeric powder, chilli powder, *garam masala* and salt and mix well.
4. Add the rice and *vaal dal* and sauté on a medium flame till the ghee coats the grains evenly.
5. Add 4 cups of hot water, stir well and pressure cook for at least 3 whistles.
6. Allow the steam to escape before opening the lid.
   Serve hot with a *raita* or *kadhi*.

RANGOON NA VAAL

Made using big Rangoon vaal beans, there is only one word to describe the look, feel and taste of this 'khatta meetha' dish YUMMY!

Preparation Time : 10 minutes.
Cooking Time : 20 minutes.
Serves 4.
Soaking Time : Overnight.

Rangoon Vaal

2 cups Rangoon *vaal* (lilva beans)
¼ tsp soda-bi-carb
¼ tsp carom seeds (*ajwain*)
¼ tsp asafoetida (*hing*)
½ tsp chilli powder
¼ tsp turmeric powder (*haldi*)
2 tbsp oil
1 tbsp grated jaggery (*gur*)
1 tsp tamarind (*imli*) pulp, optional
Salt to taste

1. Clean, wash and soak the Rangoon *vaal* in enough water overnight.
2. Drain, add the soda-bi-carb and 1½ cups of water and pressure cook for 3 to 4 whistles.
3. Allow the steam to escape before opening the lid. Keep aside.
4. Heat the oil in a *kadhai*, add the carom seeds, asafoetida, chilli powder and turmeric powder and sauté for a few minutes.
5. Add the cooked Rangoon *vaal*, 1 cup of water, jaggery, tamarind pulp and salt, mix well and simmer for 7 to 8 minutes, stirring once in between.
   Serve hot.

CHAWLI

Chawli is also known as black-eyed beans, cow peas or *lobhia*. These are small, cream-coloured beans with a black spot. They have a nutty, earthy flavour and are available fresh, canned or dried. Dried beans must be soaked and cooked.

Culinary uses: *Chawli* lends itself to a wide range of *subzis* and curries from different parts of India North to South. They are popularly cooked with coconut and curry leaves in South India; with mustard seeds or tempered with asafoetida in Gujarat; and with onions, ginger and garlic in the North. They are eaten with *rotis* and rice; and make a good, nourishing snack on toast. Combined with bland vegetables like pumpkin, they can be cooked with green chillies in coconut milk, topped with coconut oil and curry leaves, and served with steaming hot rice this is popular in Kerala and is known as Olan. Another innovative recipe is *chawli* curry wherein gram flour is added to provide a kadhi-like consistency. *Chawla masala* or *chawli* cooked in a gravy of tomatoes, spices and dried fenugreek leaves, is popular in the North.

Chawli Dal: Also known as split cow peas, they are a result of splitting regular variety of chawli. They are creamish-yellow in colour and slightly kidney bean in shape with a typical nutty flavour.

Culinary uses: *Chawli Dal* is also called *chola dal*. It is used very commonly in Gujarati snacks like *Dhokla, Panki* etc. It also goes well in a *Pulao*.

Red Chawli: Also known as red cow peas, they are small, kidney shaped beans with a black spot. It has a tough exterior which requires soaking for a few hours and then cooking. The flavour is similar to the white variety of *chawli*.

Culinary uses: Red *chawli* is tastier but not easily available. Most extensively used in making *subzis* and curries. Almost every recipe which uses the regular *chawli* can be substituted with red *chawli*.

MASALA CHAWLI

An innovative recipe of chawli or lobhia beans served in a gravy that is flavoured with tomatoes, mint and kasuri methi.

Preparation Time : 15 minutes
Cooking Time : 25 minutes.
Serves 4.
Soaking Time : 2 hours.

To be ground into a paste
¾ cup chopped mint leaves (*phudina*)
1 tsp grated ginger (*adrak*)
2 to 3 green chillies
¼ tsp lemon juice

Other ingredients
1/3 cup *chawli* (*lobhia* or black eyed beans)
2 tbsp oil
½ cup finely chopped onions
¼ cup fresh tomato pulp
¼ tsp dried fenugreek leaves (*kasuri methi*)
¼ tsp turmeric powder (*haldi*)
Salt to taste

1. Clean, wash and soak the *chawli* in enough water for at least 2 hours.
2. Drain, add 1¼ cups of water and pressure cook for 2 to 3 whistles or till they are cooked. Drain and keep aside.
3. Heat the oil in a *kadhai*, add the onions and sauté till they turn golden brown.
4. Add the tomato pulp, dried fenugreek leaves, turmeric powder and salt and cook on a slow flame till the oil separate from the gravy.
5. Add the cooked *chawli* and ½ cup of water and simmer for 4 to 5 minutes.
6. Add the prepared paste, mix well and cook for another 2 to 3 minutes. Serve hot.

KADALA CURRY

Although the main ingredient in this recipe is red chawli, it is undoubtedly the shallots or Madras onions that give this dish its unique aroma and flavour! Feast on this spicy and nutritious recipe with a bowl of steaming hot rice topped with ghee.

Preparation Time: 20 minutes.
Cooking Time: 25 minutes.
Serves 4.
Soaking Time : 3 to 4 hours.

Red Chawli

For the *masala*

3 tbsp coconut oil
½ cup sliced shallots (Madras onions)
3 whole dry Kashmiri red chillies, broken into pieces
1 tsp coriander (*dhania*) seeds
1 tsp chopped ginger (*adrak*)
¼ tsp turmeric powder (*haldi*)
½ tsp *garam masala*
½ cup freshly grated coconut
4 curry leaves (*kadi patta*)
½ tsp garlic (*lehsun*)

Other ingredients

1½ cups red *chawli* (*lobhia* /cow pea), washed and soaked for 3 to 4 hours
¼ cup sliced onions
Salt to taste
2 tsp coconut oil/any refined oil
½ tsp mustard seeds (*rai* / *sarson*)
2 curry leaves (*kadi patta*)
2 tbsp chopped shallots (Madras onions)
1 tbsp freshly grated coconut
1 whole dry Kashmiri red chilli, broken into pieces

For the *masala*

1. Heat the oil in a pan and roast all the ingredients till they release an aroma. Keep aside to cool.
2. Blend in a mixer to a fine powder and keep aside.

How to proceed

1. Combine the red *chawli* with 4 cups of water and boil till soft. Occasionally remove the froth that collects on top.
2. Add the onions, prepared *masala* and salt mix well and cook till the curry thickens. Keep aside.
3. Heat the oil in a pan, and add the mustard seeds and curry leaves.
4. When the seeds crackle, add the shallots and sauté for a minute.
5. Add the coconut and red chillies and sauté till it releases an aroma.
6. Pour the tempering on the curry and serve hot.

CHOLA DAL DHOKLA

You are sure to have tasted dhokla some time or the other, but I doubt if you would have tried this! Here is a different type of dhokla made with split cow peas, made even more visually-appealing and healthy thanks to the greens.

Preparation Time: 10 minutes.
Cooking Time: 15 minutes.
Serves 4 (Makes 16 pieces).
Soaking Time : Overnight.

½ cup *chola dal* (split cow peas)
½ cup chopped spinach (*palak*)
½ cup chopped fenugreek (*methi*) leaves
2 tsp ginger-green chilli paste
¼ tsp asafoetida (*hing*)
Salt to taste
1 tsp fruit salt
½ tsp oil for greasing

For serving
Green *chutney*

For the tempering
1 tbsp oil
1 tsp mustard seeds (*rai* / *sarson*)
8 to 10 curry leaves (*kadi patta*)
a pinch asafoetida (*hing*)

For the garnish
2 tbsp chopped coriander (*dhania*)
1 tbsp freshly grated coconut

1. Clean, wash and soak the *chola dal* in enough water overnight.
2. Drain, add the spinach, fenugreek leaves and ginger-green chilli paste and blend in a mixer to a smooth paste, adding a little water if required.
3. Add the asafoetida and salt and mix well.
4. Add the fruit salt, sprinkle a little water over it and mix gently.
5. Pour into a greased 150 mm. (6") diameter *thali* and steam for 8 to 10 minutes or till a knife inserted comes out clean.
6. For tempering, heat the oil in a small pan, add the mustard seeds, curry leaves and asafoetida and sauté till the seeds crackle. Add ¼ cup of water and mix well.
7. Pour this tempering over the *dhoklas* and cut them into 16 equal portions.
   Garnish with coriander and coconut serve with green *chutney*.

MATKI

Matki or moath beans is a pulse that is mostly consumed in the sprouted form. Also known as *mut, mot, mat,* dew beans, *matki* is very small and brownish in colour, with a creamy, yellow-coloured interior. *Matki* is similar in taste to moong beans, but has a nuttier flavour.

Culinary uses: This tiny bean, usually simmered with other vegetables and a selection of spices, is very popular in North India. *Matki* is combined with coconut in the South to give a delicious *Matki Ambat* Curry.

It is also used to make the popular *Usal* after sprouting. *Matki Pulao,* the combination of this pulse with rice is a very nutritious treat. *Matki* is also combined with vegetables like spinach to make curries, and with French beans to make healthy *subzis*. Sprouted moth beans can be used in stir-fries.

NUTRITIOUS TENDLI AND MATKI SUBZI

A thoughtful variant of the simple tendli subzi made with sprouted matki and soya granules. Soya granules enrich this subzi with its protein, calcium and iron content.

Preparation Time: 10 minutes.
Cooking Time: 15 minutes.
Serves 4.

2 tsp oil
¼ tsp cumin seeds (*jeera*)
¼ cup chopped onions
½ tsp ginger-green chilli paste
1 cup chopped round gourd (*tinda*)
½ cup sprouted *matki* (moath beans)
½ cup soya granules, soaked and drained
¼ tsp turmeric powder (*haldi*)
½ tsp chilli powder
1½ tsp coriander-cumin seed (*dhania-jeera*) powder
Salt to taste
¼ cup chopped tomatoes

For the garnish
2 tbsp chopped coriander (*dhania*)

1. Heat the oil in a pressure cooker and add the cumin seeds.
2. When the seeds crackle, add the onions and ginger-green chilli paste and sauté till the onions turn translucent.
3. Add the round gourds, *matki*, soya granules, turmeric powder, chilli powder, coriander-cumin seed powder, salt and ½ cup of water and pressure cook it for 1 to 2 whistles.
4. Allow the steam to escape before opening the lid.
5. Just before serving, add the tomatoes and mix well.
   Serve hot garnished with coriander.

VATANA

Vatana or dried peas, in some form or the other, is consumed all over the world! All thanks to their immense versatility, colour, flavour and adaptability. They make good snacks, soups and main course dishes as well. It is not surprising, then, that they are dried and kept for use all round the year. The best way to preserve peas is to dry them; this technique has been followed since many years and is a traditional method of preserving peas. They can then be soaked overnight, re-hydrated, and cooked by boiling or pressure-cooking, to be used in a variety of curries and other dishes.

There are different varieties of dried peas – green, white and black. All the three varieties are small, round and smooth. Peas, after soaking, gives out an earthy smell and flavour.

Types of vatana (dried peas)

Hara vatana: Also know as dried green peas, they are part of the legume family. They are tiny, green-coloured pods.

Culinary uses: Soaked and pressure-cooked dried green peas are combined with spices, chopped raw mangoes and grated coconut to make the popular South Indian dish sundal. Cooked peas can also be used in salads and curries; and the pureéd form is used in soups.

Safed vatana: Also know as dried white peas, these pale yellow/white coloured peas are also part of the legume family.

Culinary uses: This variety is used to make delicious salads with tomatoes and carrot. Notably, it is also used to make the popular street food, *Ragda Pattices*.

Kala vatana: Also known as dried black peas, this variety is also round and smooth and has the same earthy smell as the other two varieties.

Culinary uses: It is usually sprouted and used to make spicy *Usal* and other curries.

KOVALAM MUTTER

If you have a liking for all things tasty and spicy, this one is for you! Coconut and tomatoes combine well with peas to make an irresistible dish.

Preparation Time: 20 minutes.
Cooking Time: 45 minutes.
Serves 4.
Soaking Time : 2 to 3 hours.

Hara Vatana

3 tbsp oil
½ tsp cumin seeds (*jeera*)
1 tsp *urad dal* (split black gram)
4 to 5 curry leaves (*kadi patta*)
¼ cup chopped onions
1 tbsp ginger-garlic (*adrak-lehsun*) paste
1 tsp coriander-cumin seed (*dhania-jeera*) powder
1 tsp chilli powder
½ tsp turmeric powder (*haldi*)
¾ cup chopped tomatoes
Salt to taste
2 cups soaked and cooked *hara vatana* (dried green peas)

To be ground into a smooth paste
4 tbsp grated fresh coconut
2 tbsp broken cashewnuts (*kaju*), soaked and drained
2 tsp of water

For the garnish
2 tbsp chopped coriander (*dhania*)

1. Heat the oil in a *kadhai* and add the cumin seeds and *urad dal*.
2. When the seeds crackle, add the curry leaves and onions and sauté till the onions turn translucent.
3. Add the ginger-garlic paste and sauté again for a few seconds.
4. Add the coriander-cumin seed powder, chilli powder and turmeric powder, tomatoes and salt and sauté for 2 to 3 minutes, while stirring continuously.
5. Add the coconut-cashewnut paste and sauté for another minute, while stirring continuously.
6. Add ¾ cup of water and bring to boil.
7. Add the *hara vatana* and simmer for another 3 to 4 minutes.
   Serve hot garnished with coriander.

RAGDA PATTIES

What better way to consume white peas than in the form of an ever-favourite street-food and that too when it comes in a healthy version!

Preparation Time: 15 minutes.
Cooking Time: 25 minutes.
Serves 4.
Soaking Time: Overnight.

For the *ragda*
1 cup *safed vatana* (dried white peas), soaked overnight
Salt to taste
1 tbsp oil
1 tsp mustard seeds (*rai / sarson*)
6 to 7 curry leaves (*kadi patta*)
A pinch asafoetida (*hing*)
¼ cup turmeric powder (*haldi*)
½ tsp chilli powder
2 tsp ginger-green chilli paste
1 tbsp grated jaggery (*gur*)
1 tbsp tamarind (*imli*) pulp

For the potato mixture
2 cups boiled and mashed potatoes
2 tsp cornflour
Salt to taste
Oil for cooking

To be mixed into a stuffing
3 tbsp freshly grated coconut
3 tbsp chopped coriander (*dhania*)
¼ tsp finely chopped green chillies
1 tsp sugar
Salt to taste

For serving
½ cup *khajur imli chutney*
¼ cup green *chutney*
4 tbsp chopped onions

For the garnish
2 tbsp chopped coriander (*dhania*)

For the *ragda*

1. Drain the *safed vatana*, add 1 cup of water, salt and pressure cook for 4 whistles.
2. Heat the oil in a *kadhai* and add the mustard seeds, curry leaves and asafoetida.
3. When the seeds crackle, add all the remaining ingredients and 1¼ cups of water and mix well.
4. Mash the peas slightly so that the gravy thickens and simmer for 10 minutes. Keep aside.

For the stuffed *patties*

1. Combine the potatoes, cornflour and salt together in a bowl and mix well.
2. Divide into 8 equal portions and keep aside.
3. On a flat dry surface roll out each portion into a 75 mm. (3") diameter circle patting using your hands. Place 1½ tsp of the stuffing in the centre.
4. Bring together the edges in the centre to seal the filling inside the potato circle.
5. Repeat with the remaining potato mixture and stuffing to make 7 more stuffed *patties*.
6. Cook them on a non-stick pan, using a little oil till both sides turn golden brown in colour. Keep aside.

How to proceed

1. Place 2 *patties* on a serving plate and pour ¼th portion of the *ragda* over it.
2. Pour 2 tbsp of *khajur imli chutney*, 1 tbsp of green *chutney* and 1 tbsp of onions on top.
3. Repeat with the remaining *patties* and *ragda* to make 3 more servings.

   Serve hot garnished with coriander.

PUMPKIN KOOTTU CURRY

Even those who otherwise find vegetables like pumpkin to be bland cannot resist this interestingly seasoned curry, all thanks to the crunch of kala vatana!

Preparation Time: 15 minutes.
Cooking Time: 25 minutes.
Serves 6.
Soaking Time : Overnight.

To be ground into a smooth paste (makes approx. ¾ cup)

¾ cup freshly grated coconut
8 whole dry Kashmiri red chillies, broken into pieces
1 tsp cumin seeds (*jeera*)
¼ cup of water

Other ingredients

¼ cup *kala vatana* (dried black peas)
Salt to taste
2½ cups chopped red pumpkin (*bhopla /kaddu*)
1 tbsp coconut oil / any other refined oil
1 tsp mustard seeds (*rai / sarson*)
2 tsp *urad dal* (split black gram)

For the garnish

8 to 10 curry leaves (*kadi patta*)

1. Soak the *kala vatana* in enough water overnight or for at least 5 to 6 hours.
2. Drain, add 1 cup of water and pressure cook for 3 to 4 whistles.
3. Allow the steam to escape before opening the lid.
4. Add the pumpkin, 1 cup of water and salt, mix well and cook on a medium flame for 10 to 12 minutes, while stirring occasionally.
5. Add the prepared paste, mix gently and simmer for 5 to 7 minutes. Keep aside.
6. For the tempering, heat the oil in small pan and add the mustard seeds.
7. When the seeds crackle, add the *urad dal* and sauté for few seconds.
8. Pour this tempering over the curry and mix well.
   Serve hot garnished with curry leaves.

RAJMA

Beans are an inexpensive source of protein. One of the most popular beans is *rajma* or kidney bean, which is so named because of its shape. *Rajma* is an inseparable part of Punjabi cuisine. You are sure to have heard of the ever-popular *rajma chawal* a meal of rice and *rajma* curry that is consumed on festive occasions as well on a regular basis. There are different types of *rajma* and one can easily be substituted for the other.

Types of Rajma

Red Rajma:

These are available in two colours. The first one being large, with a deep reddish-brown colour, and the most common type of kidney bean available in India.

The other one is the shaded *rajma*. which is light pink in colour with reddish spots and are a quite versatile and commonly used in Punjabi and Mexican cuisine.

Kashmiri beans: These are deep red in colour with properties similar to red kidney beans. The only difference is that they are smaller in size. They retain their shape when cooked and are more popular in Kashmiri cuisines, soups, salads and curries.

Culinary Uses of Rajma: In addition to the ever favourite *rajma chawal*, kidney beans are also used in a variety of other dishes; for example, they can be added to numerous salads like the Three-bean Salad and soups like Spicy Bean and Tomato Soup. Kidney beans are also popular in Mexican cuisine; in fact, the famous tacos are stuffed with kidney beans in a tomato sauce. *Rajma* can also be used as a stuffing to make nutritious *parathas*.

TORTILLA BAKE

Wholesome and a filling recipe made using tortillas, vegetables, rajma and yummy white sauce. Serve this to your guests and win all the praises.

Preparation Time: 30 minutes.
Cooking Time: 1 hour.
Serves 4.
Baking Temperature: 200 °C (400 °F)
Baking Time: 20 minutes.
Soaking Time: Overnight.

For the tortillas
¾ cup maize flour *(makai ka atta)*
¾ cup plain flour *(maida)*
4 tsp oil
¾ tsp salt

For the refried beans
2 tbsp butter
2 tbsp oil
½ cup sliced onions
1 clove garlic (*lehsun*)
3 green chillies, finely chopped
1 cup red *rajma* (kidney beans), soaked overnight
1 cup chopped tomatoes
2 tsp sugar
1 tsp roasted cumin seeds (*jeera*) powder
Salt to taste

For the vegetable layer
1 tbsp oil
½ cup sliced onions
¼ cup chopped capsicum
½ cup sweet corn kernels (*makai ke dane*)
1 cup sliced mushrooms (*khumbh*)
1 tsp Tabasco sauce
Salt and freshly ground pepper to taste

For the white sauce
1 tbsp butter
1 tbsp plain flour *(maida)*
1 cup milk
Salt and freshly ground pepper to taste

Other ingredients
½ tsp butter for greasing

For the garnish
½ cup grated cheese

For the tortillas

1. Combine both the flours, oil and salt in a bowl and mix well.
2. Add enough warm water and knead into a soft dough.
3. Divide the dough into 3 equal portions and roll out each portion into a circle of 175 mm. (7") diameter.
4. Cook each dough circle on a *tava* (griddle) lightly on both the sides and keep aside.

For the refried beans

1. Heat the butter and oil in a pressure cooker, add the onions and sauté till the onions translucent, while stirring continuously.
2. Add the garlic and green chillies and sauté for a few more seconds.
3. Add all the remaining ingredients and pressure cook for 4 to 5 whistles or till the *rajma* are cooked.
4. Allow the steam to escape before opening the lid. Keep aside to cool.
5. Mash lightly with a spoon and keep aside.

For the vegetable layer

1. Heat the oil in a deep pan, add the onions and sauté till the onions turns translucent, while stirring continuously.
2. Add the onions, capsicum, corn and mushrooms, mix well and cook on a medium flame till the mushrooms turn soft.

3. Add the Tabasco sauce, salt and pepper and mix well. Keep aside.

For the white sauce

1. Heat the butter in a deep pan, add the flour and cook on a slow flame until froth appears, while stirring continuously.
2. Add the milk gradually and stir continuously until the sauce thickens.
3. Add the salt and pepper and mix well. Keep aside.

How to proceed

1. Grease a 200 mm. (8″) ovenproof dish lightly with butter.
2. Place one tortilla at the bottom of the dish and spread the refried beans over the tortilla.
3. Place another tortilla on top and spread the vegetable layer evenly over it.
4. Finally place the third tortilla on top and pour the white sauce evenly over it.
5. Garnish with grated cheese and bake in a pre-heated oven at 200°C (400°F) for 15 minutes. Serve hot.

RAJMA SALAD

This Mexican flavoured salad is sure to impress your guests and its easy to make too.

Preparation Time : 10 minutes.
Cooking Time : Nil.
Serves 4.
Soaking Time: Overnight.

Shaded Rajma

To be mixed together into a dressing
½ cup blanched, peeled and finely chopped tomatoes
½ cup finely chopped spring onion whites
2 tbsp finely chopped coriander (*dhania*)
½ tsp finely chopped green chilles
Salt and sugar to taste

For the garnish
2 tbsp grated cheese
1 cherry tomato, halves

Other ingredients
1 cup soaked overnight and cooked shaded *rajma* (kidney beans)
3 to 4 cherry tomatoes, cut into halves
¼ cup *paneer* (cottage cheese) cubes
¼ cup cooked sweet corn kernels (*makai ke dane*)
¼ cup chopped capsicum
¼ cup crushed nachos (readily available in the market)
2 tbsp finely chopped spring onion greens
Salt to taste
2 tbsp grated cheese

1. Combine all the ingredients together in a salad bowl. Keep refrigerated.
2. Just before serving add the dressing and toss well.
   Serve immediately garnished with cheese and cherry tomatoes.

RAJMA CURRY

A world-famous recipe from the kitchens of Punjab, this is not just delicious but also wholesome and filling when served with chawal.

Preparation Time : 5 minutes.
Cooking Time : 30 minutes.
Serves 4.
Soaking Time : Overnight.

Kashmiri Rajma

¾ cup Kashmiri *rajma* (kidney beans), soaked overnight
2 tbsp oil
½ tsp cumin seeds (*jeera*)
25mm. (1″) stick cinnamon (*dalchini*)
½ cup sliced onions
1 tbsp thinly sliced ginger (*adrak*)
2 green chillies, slit
¼ tsp turmeric powder (*haldi*)
2 tbsp coriander (*dhania*) powder
Salt to taste
1½ tbsp dry mango powder (*amchur*)
½ tsp black salt (*sanchal*)

For the garnish
2 tbsp chopped coriander (*dhania*)
2 tsp ginger juliens

1. Drain the water from the *rajma*, wash and keep aside.
2. Heat the oil in a pressure cooker and add the cumin seeds and cinnamon.
3. When the seeds crackle, add the onions and sauté on a medium flame till they turn translucent, while stirring continuously.
4. Add the ginger and green chillies and sauté for a few more minutes.
5. Add the *rajma*, turmeric powder, coriander powder, salt and 3 cups of water, mixed well and pressure cook for 4 to 5 whistles.
6. Allow the steam to escape before opening the lid.
7. Add the dry mango powder and black salt, mix well and simmer for a few more minutes, stirring once in between.

   Serve hot garnished with coriander and ginger juliens.

LESSER-KNOWN DALS

While compiling information about various *dals* I came across *dals* that were unknown or often ignored. Yet, these *dals* play an important role in our cuisine and also have added nutritional benefits.

KULITH

Horse gram, also known as *gahat*, *kulath* or *kulith*, is a small, flat, oval bean with a darkish rusty-tan colour and an assertive earthy flavour. Horse gram is an excellent source of iron and molybdenum.

Culinary Uses: It is sprouted and used in curries and stir-fries, and also made into thick soups. *Kulith* is consumed as a whole seed or as sprouts by a large rural population in South India and is also a major ingredient in the Pahadi cuisine of Himalayas. It is also made into flour and used to make *rotis, dosas*, etc. The stock obtained by cooking *kulith* in water can be tempered with garlic and dry red chillies and consumed as soup.

KULITH SAAR

A famous Manglorean recipe cooked like Osaman of Gujarati cuisine.

Preparation Time : 5 minutes.
Cooking Time : 20 minutes.
Serves 4.
Soaking Time : Overnight.

Kulith

¼ cup *Kulith* (horse gram), soaked overnight
Salt to taste
2 tbsp oil
½ tsp mustard seeds (*rai / sarson*)
1 whole dry Kashmiri red chilli, broken into pieces
¼ tsp asafoetida (*hing*)
6-7 curry leaves (*kadi patta*)

1. Clean, wash and soak the *kulith* in enough water overnight.
2. Drain the *kulith,* add 4 cups of water and salt and cook for 20-25 minutes on a medium flame till the *kulith* gets over cooked.
3. Mash it lightly with the back of a spoon and keep aside.
4. For the tempering, heat the oil in a small pan and add the mustard seeds.
5. When mustard seeds crackle, add the red chillies, asafoetida and curry leaves and sauté for 30 seconds pour this tempering over the prepared *saar* and mix well.
   Serve piping hot with steamed rice.

BLACK BEANS

Also known as black Spanish beans, common beans, Tampico beans, turtle beans and Venezuelan beans, the black bean is said to have originated in southern Mexico and central America over 7000 years ago, but today it is used all over the world. This small bean has a cream-coloured flesh covered in a black skin. It has a slightly sweet flavour and a mealy texture. You get dried black beans as well as pre-cooked and canned black beans in the market, but these are not readily available in India.

Culinary Uses: They can be used to make soups, stews and sauces.

BLACK BEAN SOUP

A traditional mildly flavored Mexican soup.

Preparation Time : 10 minutes.
Cooking Time : 25 to 30 minutes.
Serves 6.
Soaking Time : 6 to 8 hours.

Black Beans

¾ cup black beans
4 large tomatoes, cut into quarters
2 cloves garlic (*lehsun*)
2 tbsp butter
¼ cup chopped onions
Salt to taste

For serving
Toasted bread

1. Clean, wash and soak the black beans in enough water for 6 to 8 hours and drain well.
2. Add 5 cups of water, tomatoes and garlic and pressure cook for 2 whistles.
3. Allow the steam to escape before opening the lid and keep aside.
4. When cool, blend in a mixer till a smooth. Do not strain the mixture. Keep aside.
5. Heat the butter in a deep non-stick pan, add the onions and sauté till the onions turn translucent, while stirring continuously.
6. Add the black bean purée and salt and simmer for a another 3 to 4 minutes, stirring once in between.

   Serve hot with toasted bread.

HARICOT BEANS

This small, dry, white, oval-shaped French bean is often used to make baked bean dishes. It is also referred to as Boston beans, Boston navy beans, navy beans, haricot beans (white), or pearl haricot beans.

Haricot beans are very nutritious and filling, but not readily available in India, except as tinned baked beans (which is available in super markets).

Baked Beans

Culinary Uses: These beans are probably best-known in the form of 'Baked Beans' where the cooked beans are covered in tomato sauce. It is a common ingredient used in soups and salads. Probably best-known in the form of 'Baked Beans' where the cooked beans are covered in tomato sauce. It is a common ingredient used in soups and salads.

MACARONI HOT POT

A pasta treat that goes well as the perfect recipe for entertaining your guests. Macaroni, a type of pasta that is combined with onions and capsicum, tossed in tomato purée and served topped with cheese is sure to win its fans.

Preparation Time : 10 minutes.
Cooking Time : 15 minutes.
Serves 4.
Baking Temperature: 200 °C (400 °F).
Baking Time : 25 minutes.

Haricot Beans

4 tbsp butter
¾ cup onion rings
1½ cups capsicum rings
1 tbsp crushed or grated garlic (*lehsun*)
8 to 9 medium tomatoes, blanched and chopped
2 tsp chilli powder
4 cups cooked macaroni
1 large can baked beans
¼ cup tomato ketchup
1 tsp sugar
Salt to taste
1 cup grated cooking cheese for topping

1. Heat the butter in a deep pan, add the onions and sauté on a medium flame for 2 to 3 minutes, while stirring continuously.
2. Add the capsicum, mix well gently and sauté on a medium flame for 2 to 3 minutes, while stirring continuously.
3. Remove a few onion and capsicum rings and keep aside for garnishing.
4. Add the garlic, tomatoes and chilli powder, mix well and cook on a medium flame for 5 minutes, while stirring continuously.
5. Add the macaroni, beans, tomato ketchup, sugar and salt, toss gently and cover and cook on a slow flame for another 2 to 3 minutes.
6. Remove from the flame, sprinkle the cheese evenly over it and garnish with sautéed onion and capsicum rings.
7. Cover and bake in a pre-heated oven at 200°C (400°F) for 20 minutes or till the cheese melts. Serve hot.